MOMENT BY MOMENT

MOMENT BY MOMENT

THE ART AND PRACTICE OF MINDFULNESS

JERRY BRAZA, Ph.D.

FOREWORD BY THICH NHAT HANH
NOBEL PEACE PRIZE NOMINEE

CHARLES E. TUTTLE, CO., INC.
Boston • Rutland, Vermont • Tokyo

First published in 1997 by Tuttle Publishing,
an imprint of Periplus Editions (HK) Ltd.,
with editorial offices at 153 Milk Street,
Boston, Massachusetts 02109.

Copyright © 1997 Jerry Braza

Library of Congress Cataloging-in-Publication Data

Braza, Jerry, 1944–
    Moment by moment : the art and practice of mindfulness / Jerry Braza ;
foreword by Thich Nhat Hanh.
    p. cm.
    Includes bibliographical references.
    ISBN 0-8048-3113-0
    1. Meditation. 2. Attention. 3. Ānāpānasmrti. 4. Conduct of life. I. Title.
    BF637.M4B73 1997
    158.1—dc21
                                                                97-4179
                                                                CIP

DISTRIBUTED BY

USA
Charles E. Tuttle Co., Inc.
RR 1 Box 231-5
North Clarendon, VT 05759
(800) 526-2778

Japan
Tuttle Shokai Ltd.
1-21-13, Seki
Tama-ku, Kawasaki-shi 214
Japan
(044) 833-0225
Fax (044) 822-0413

Southeast Asia
Berkeley Books Pte Ltd
5 Little Road #08-01
Singapore 536983
(65) 280-3320
Fax (65) 280-6290

First Edition
05 04 03 02 01 00 99   3 5 7 9 10 8 6 4

Design by Kathryn Sky-Peck
PRINTED IN THE UNITED STATES OF AMERICA

We can only be said to be alive
in those moments when our hearts
are conscious of our treasures.

—THORNTON WILDER

CONTENTS

PART ONE: AN OVERVIEW

PART TWO: THE PROCESS

PART THREE: APPLICATIONS OF MINDFULNESS

Part Four: Maintaining a Mindful Lifestyle

FOREWORD

MINDFULNESS IS THE BASIS for transforming ourselves and creating a more harmonious family and society. It is the miracle that allows us to become fully alive in each moment. The deepest fruit of mindfulness practice is the realization that peace and joy are available, within us and around us, right here and now. This is something we can taste, and we can offer it to everyone we meet and everyone we love.

In *Moment by Moment*, Dr. Jerry Braza suggests many simple exercises in which to apply the practice of mindfulness to our daily lives. I congratulate him for offering such thoughtful, creative, and clear explanations of the practical benefits of practicing mindfulness. This is a very useful guide for living mindfully. I hope you will return to it again and again and practice wholeheartedly the exercises Dr. Braza offers.

THICH NHAT HANH
PLUM VILLAGE, FRANCE

ACKNOWLEDGMENTS

THIS BOOK REFLECTS DAILY interactions and relationships with family, friends, and, in particular, my wife Kathleen. With her help I have an ongoing opportunity to practice mindfulness moment by moment. Her love, support, and encouragement have provided a mirror for my own struggle of living mindfully. In addition, she has provided the editorial critique that has kept me focused.

I appreciate my daughter Andrea, and son Mark, who loved me despite my earlier years of "mindless" and hurried living. Now as adults they have provided a validation for my more mindful lifestyle. I appreciate my friends who have offered feedback regarding this project and the Salt Lake City Sangha for their support and friendship. I'm thankful to Becky Jones and Toni Mertin for their help in editing and designing the first edition of this book. Special appreciation goes to Isabelle Bleecker, my editor in this edition. Her own practice of mindfulness, as well as her insight and clarity, offered me wonderful support and belief in this work. Thanks are also due to my students at Western Oregon State College who provided suggestions for this latest edition and who are daily reminders that my life needs to be my message.

I also acknowledge my mother, Genevieve, who mindfully watches the apple tree bloom, produce, and shed its leaves outside her apartment window. Mom, thanks for all the moments that you shared with me and for your ongoing love and support.

INTRODUCTION

YOU ARE ABOUT TO DISCOVER, and hopefully begin to experience, one of the oldest and most profound strategies for enhancing health, relationships, productivity, and happiness—*mindfulness*.

Mindfulness is the practice of becoming fully aware of each moment and one's experience of that moment. Rooted in ancient traditions, this practice is being used successfully today at mind-body clinics nationwide.

Early in my life, I tended to live for the next moment. I was the type of individual who would skip pages when reading bedtime stories to my children. On family vacations, my primary focus was to get there, so rarely was the journey itself very enjoyable. Through meditation (which simply means "to attend to"), I began to transform my way of looking at life. My experience has been that most people tend to enjoy life less because they often miss it along the way. Life is everything we miss while we are making other plans.

After a critical review of the literature in the field of health and psychology, I discovered virtually hundreds of different strategies for achieving well-being and happiness. However, it became clear to me that no single technique or process is the magic pill for managing stress or the other life problems we experience. Consequently, I became more interested in exploring the philosophies and approaches that can help individuals live more fully, both at home and in the workplace. I invite you to consider the *quality* of your experience moment by moment as a practical and even unique barometer of a healthy and successful life. The practice of mindfulness is one way to begin this adventure.

The materials in this book are based on the Mindfulness Training Program that I have created and conducted for individuals from various professions who want to experience life more fully. The program is the result of my experiences with teachers like Carl Rogers, who taught me the value of presence; Elisabeth Kübler-Ross, who impressed upon me the importance of completing unfinished business; Beata Jencks, who stressed awareness and breathing in her mind-body work; Ram Dass, Stephen Levine, and Jack Kornfield, who introduced me to the practice of meditation; and especially to Thich Nhat Hanh, who continues to inspire me with his mindful presence, teachings, and ongoing contributions to individual and world peace. This is not just another book on managing stress, although mindfulness provides a fundamental way of coping with that problem. My goal is to help you recall what you already know and reawaken your spirit to the beauty and joy that exist in every moment.

Moment by Moment can become a tool that helps you learn how to regain that natural state of joy and discovery so recognizable in young children, that state of appreciation for each moment as it is experienced for the first time. Learning to become more mindful provides an alternative to living *mindlessly* or mechanically.

Moment by Moment can also remind you of the preciousness of each moment and help you realize that the next moment could possibly be your last. This book offers a process and applications that help you experience the most routine activities, such as breathing, eating, and walking, with joy. This process can practically become a way of being that can reduce stress, enhance productivity and relationships, and create joy. The reader is encouraged to use this book as a companion and guide to mindful living. Take time to pause, reflect, and practice the exercises along the way. Learning to be is as important as learning to *do*.

Right now, in this moment, pause and appreciate your breath and aliveness. In this moment, there is health, wholeness, and the potential for joy and peace. Through this simple awareness of your breath and the present moment, you have already begun a process that hopefully you will practice and experience *moment by moment*.

As we begin this journey into mindfulness, I invite you to reflect upon the following questions. These questions can only be answered by looking deeply within yourself, a process addressed throughout this book.

1. What am I missing while I am making other plans?

2. Where am I going anyway?

3. How would I complete the following statements?
    "I'll be happy when_____"
    "If only_____"

4. What from the past is robbing me of a sense of peace?

5. How often am I with someone yet not really there?

6. How often do I live in the present moment?

7. What keeps me from living in the present moment?

8. What pleasurable things am I attached to?

9. What painful things do I deny?

10. What am I "hanging on" to?

11. What pleasures have I failed to enjoy?

12. What are the optimum conditions for my personal growth?

13. In what ways can I become more peaceful?

14. Who are the happiest people I know?

15. What is their secret?

16. What kind of experiences/activities provide me with the greatest joy?

17. In what moments of my life am I most alive?

18. Am I a "human doing" or a "human **be**ing?"

19. What are the optimum conditions for really being with another person?

20. In what ways do I live my life "mindlessly" or robotically?

A core question is the question or issue of greatest relevance to an individual. From the list above, select your own core question and write it below:

_____

_____

Moment by Moment offers insights into these and many more questions that pertain to living your life in a more mindful and awakened way.

PART ONE

An Overview

I have learned to be happy where I am. I have learned that locked within the moments of each day are all the joys, the peace, the fibers of the cloth we call life. The meaning is in the moment. There is no other way to find it. You feel what you allow yourself to feel, each and every moment of the day.

—RUSS BERRIE

IN PART ONE, YOU WILL

- Discover the meaning of mindfulness

- Develop a mind-set for developing mindfulness

- Learn the importance of mindfulness in your life

- Take the Mindfulness Test

WHAT
IS
MINDFULNESS?

MINDFULNESS IS A NATURAL state of living moment by moment. Observe young children, and you will quickly notice that the majority of their awareness is in the present moment. They are not concerned with past or future. I recall a time driving my young children somewhere when we approached a railroad crossing as the lights began to flash and the safety gate went down. My first thought was "Oh no! We're going to be held up by a train and be late." Just then, my daughter called out from the backseat, "Daddy, Daddy, we're so lucky! We get to watch the train go by!" Her awareness of the present moment was a wonderful reminder to stop and enjoy what this journey had to offer along the way. Young children can be our teachers of mindfulness as they take delight in the tiny bug crawling on a leaf, the sound of a fish splashing in the stream, and the feel of the sand beneath their feet rather than the "total picture," so to speak.

This same awareness is also observable in the elderly or in individuals who are close to death. My neighbor, John, terminally ill with cancer, cherished each evening sunset shared with his wife on the front porch and often expressed a new and profound sense of beauty for and appreciation of his garden and backyard mountain view. Recognition of the preciousness of each moment is more apparent in those who *know* the end of life as we know it is near. As author Joan Borysenko states, "We are all terminal; the question is not whether we will die but how we are going to live."

Mindfulness has many definitions, some of which go back thousands of years:

> *Mindfulness refers to keeping one's*
> *consciousness alive to the present reality.*
> *It is the miracle by which we master and*
> *restore ourselves.*
>
> —THICH NHAT HANH

> *Mindfulness is a state in which one is open to creating categories, open to new information, and being aware of more than one perspective. Mindlessness is being prematurely bound to a perspective when in a particular situation and then acting from that particular mindset.*
>
> —ELLEN LANGER

> *Mindfulness is an ancient Asian technique, dating back to classical Buddhism in India. It is still practiced in its early form in certain countries, particularly Burma and Thailand. For centuries, the Japanese started to apply Zen awareness to tea-making, proof of how mindfulness can be used in daily routines.*
> *Currently, mindfulness is being used as a healing tool in Western medicine.*
>
> —DANIEL GOLEMAN AND TARA BENNETT-GOLEMAN

In the Western traditions, mindfulness is associated with devotional practices in which the Divine is a constant companion within us. In Christianity, the practice is having Jesus by our side at all times. In Judaism, the cabalistic idea that creation is taking place in each and every moment brings an acute sensitivity to everything. All of these ideas can be practiced to raise our level of awareness and induce an entirely new perspective, seeing things "as they really are."
—DAVID COOPER

Mindfulness is a technique that teaches intent alertness. It means becoming fully aware of each moment and of your activity in that moment. It is living each moment, in contrast to "mindlessness," which means that you allow your mind to get "hooked" or attached to thoughts and desires that arise at random.

Does any of this sound familiar to you? Although you may not have called it mindfulness, the concept is similar to contemplation, prayer, meditation, martial arts, or yoga, to name a few. All of these practices are based on attention. Growing up Catholic, I practiced repetitive prayers in a ritual known as "saying the rosary." Later, I experimented with a variety of Eastern meditative practices. Through these experiences, I often found serenity and peace in the moment. Although it may merely be a question of semantics, the ingredients of mindfulness are found in most religious traditions and practices.

In general, meditation is based on attention to the workings of the mind, whereas prayer is based on attention to the presence of the sacred in life. According to Rick Fields in *Chop Wood, Carry Water*, "The martial arts, Hatha Yoga, and spiritual dance are based on attention to spirit moving through the body. And the disciplines of inner guidance are based on attention to the wisdom of the 'still, small voice within.'" A common theme in all of these practices is mindfulness.

There are two important qualities of the mindfulness process. The first is that of living in the present moment, and the latter is related to keeping oneself open to a variety of perspectives. After I shared the concept of mindfulness with a friend, he wrote on a piece of paper the following familiar statement and asked me to read it aloud:

> *"I love Paris in the*
> *the spring."*

My first, second, and third responses were, "I love Paris in the spring." However, in reading the statement again mindfully, I noticed the extra word *the* in the sentence! This is a simple illustration of how you can become caught on one familiar way of viewing something or someone and therefore move through life clinging to one safe and familiar pattern, unaware of the incredible variety of options and perspectives available to you on your life journey. It is easy to see how you can become trapped in a fairly robotic way of living as you travel the same route to work, respond to others in routine ways, and repetitively perform daily tasks. I will often ask my students to list all of the mind*less* activities that they have engaged in that day. Their lists tend to reflect the boredom and lack of zest and excitement that comprise a good portion of their day. By learning to wake up to all of the options in the present moment and to let go of old models and ways of being in the world, they immediately begin to discover new meaning and joy in life.

MIND-SET FOR MINDFULNESS

DEVELOPING MINDFULNESS, like any new behavior, requires a different mind-set. Jon Kabat-Zinn, founder of the University of Massachusetts Medical Center's Stress Reduction Clinic, advocates seven attitudinal foundations of mindfulness: "They are non-judging, patience, a beginner's mind, trust, non-striving, acceptance, and letting go." To help you develop a mind-set for mindfulness, consider the following:

- Are you able to observe your thoughts without judging? How often do you judge yourself rather than simply observe the thoughts as they arise? Learning to be unconditionally accepting of others begins with being *non-judgmental* of yourself.

- Do you seek instant pain relief and instant pleasure, rather than allowing events to occur at their own pace and time? A complete openness to each moment requires *patience*.

- Do you consider yourself an expert or a beginner? From Zen philosophy comes the notion of the *beginner's mind*, which means that you are learning to experience each moment and activity as if it were for the first time. Children provide excellent models of this concept.

- How often do you wait for others to decide before making a personal decision? Learning to *trust* yourself rather than looking to others is a key to developing mindfulness. In the process of observing thoughts, feelings, sensations, and bodily experience, you learn to trust that as everything in nature changes, so will the experience of the moment change.

- Most of our waking day is spent in "doing" or striving to go somewhere or get something. Non-striving infers "being," and striving infers "doing." Creating some time each day to just "be" is difficult, since most of our identity is often based on what we do or what gets done. Developing a proper mind-set for mindfulness requires an awareness of being open to anything and everything that is experienced. Learning to be happy in the moment and finding a time to "be" each day without constant striving is at the heart of the mindfulness practice.

- Do you have a hard time accepting yourself? In practicing mindfulness, you accept each moment as it comes, and you are with it fully. *Acceptance* is learned as you observe the thoughts, feelings, sensations, and experiences that arise without judgment. Learning to accept your past, despite the pain, failures, and problems, will be difficult unless you learn to accept what is happening in the present.

- How often do you "hang on" to experiences and people from the past? Forgiveness means *letting go.* One of my favorite quotes is "Hanging on to resentment is allowing someone you despise to live rent free in your head." If you can observe and let go of the thoughts, feelings, sensations, and experiences that arise from moment to moment, it will be easier to let go of the past.

Look at your everyday relationships, for example. Naturally, if you tend to be *judgmental* or lack *patience*, how can you expect to truly *accept* others? If you always have to be right or be the expert, how can you learn from others around you? If you cannot let go of the past or seem to be always striving for the future, how can you possibly experience others in the here and now? As you learn to become more mindful, there are many profound insights you can gain about yourself and your relationship with others. As you progress with the practice of mindfulness, you will learn to personalize what mindfulness means to you and apply this mind-set to your daily life.

Reflections

To live without mindfulness is to live as if we were dead already.
—SHARON SALZBERG

In the beginner's mind there are many possibilities, but in the expert's, there are few.
—SHUNRYU SUZUKI

You don't have to do anything. Nowhere to go, nothing to do.
Be peaceful with the way things are now, relax, let go.
—ANONYMOUS

For everything there is a season,
And a time for every matter under heaven:
A time to be born, and a time to die,
A time to kill, and a time to heal,
A time to weep, and a time to laugh;
A time to mourn, and a time to dance,
A time to keep, and a time to cast away . . .
—ECCLESIASTES

I have learned that my total organismic sensing of a situation is more trustworthy than my intellect.
—CARL ROGERS

- What does the word *mindfulness* mean to you?

- Allow yourself time to focus on thoughts as they arise. How many are based on judgment?

- In what ways in your daily life might you use the concepts described in "Mind-set for Mindfulness?"

WHY
MINDFULNESS?

S EVERAL YEARS AGO I ATTENDED a workshop presented by Dr. Elisabeth Kübler-Ross, the famous physician who has been a pioneer in our understanding of death and dying. What I remember most from this experience were the stories that she shared about her work with the dying. After working with thousands of dying patients, Dr. Kübler-Ross observed that what most people remember most at the end of their lives were *moments.* Business, work, deadlines, bills, degrees, possessions, all assume little or no importance to the dying person in comparison to special moments with loved ones. On a trip to Southern California with my then five-year-old daughter, we spent time at the typical tourist attractions. We also spent some time walking on the beach and writing notes to each other in the sand. A short time after returning, I asked my daughter what she enjoyed most about the trip. Thinking she would say "Disneyland!," I was surprised and moved by her statement, "The best part was walking down the beach with you, Dad." So whether a person is close to death or living as a child does, what really seems to matter are *moments.* To live more moments as if they were our first or our last may itself provide enough motivation to become more mindful. But mindfulness offers even more benefits.

Stress reduction. Sixty to ninety percent of all illness may be directly or indirectly related to stress, and stress reduction is a major concern in today's world. Often stress is the result of being over-committed or having a tendency to always hurry. Living in the moment may clearly be one of the best-kept secrets for effective stress reduction and wellness. According to a family practice physician, "When the waiting room and all the examining rooms are full, my best coping strategy is to become completely mindful of the person I am with."

Increased productivity. Effectiveness and productivity are enhanced when a person's concentration is improved. When the mind wanders, it is difficult to concentrate. Preoccupation with the past or the future, coupled with "polyphasic thinking" (many thoughts at one time), results in unfulfilled activities, tasks, and relationships. Studies have shown that by developing mindfulness, individuals can concentrate more effectively and thus become more productive. Often my students will validate the relevance of mindfulness in staying focused in order to complete their work on time.

Enhanced relationships. Think about the most important people in your life and recall the last interactions you had with them. Were you really *with* them? Whether personally or professionally, our presence speaks louder than words. A nursing supervisor recently realized that as she interacted with her colleagues, she was usually working on charting and other tasks at the same time. By truly being present and attentive, you let the other person know that he or she is most important to you in that moment. The best gift you can give to another is the gift of your full presence.

Joy. In our attempts to hurry, we frequently miss the opportunity to enjoy the little pleasures that are happening moment by moment. How many sunsets, smiles, and small adventures have you missed? As you develop the skill and art of mindfulness, you can learn to work and play in a less frantic, more enjoyable, and more focused manner. The result is inevitably the experience of more joy in your life.

Peace. Violence is one of society's top concerns today. National and local governments desperately seek strategies to curb the onslaught of violent behavior with gun control laws, curfews, stricter penalties, and more prisons. Yet the solution really lies in each and every one of us. The current Dalai Lama, a Nobel Peace Prize recipient, has said, "When we have inner peace, we can be at peace with those around us." To be peaceful requires a practice or a way of being that can break the cycle of violence and hatred so pervasive in many parts of our lives. The practice of mindfulness can help us discover the path to peace.

Reflections

*Nothing can be more useful to a man or woman than
a determination not to be hurried.*

—ANONYMOUS

*The flower, the sky, your beloved can only be found
in the present moment.*

—THICH NHAT HANH

*Most men pursue pleasure with such breathless haste
they hurry past it.*

—SØREN KIERKEGAARD

- Think of one stressful problem in your life today. How might the practice of mindfulness help to reduce the distress (negative consequences) of the problem?

- Explore areas in your life in which you are not as productive as you would like to be. How might the practice of mindfulness enhance your concentration and productivity in your personal and professional life?

- Think of one person who you often take for granted. How might the practice of mindfulness bring new vitality to that relationship?

- What joyful moments in your life can you be sure to capture today?

- How can you create more peaceful moments in your life?

MINDFULNESS TEST

To EXPLORE THE CONCEPT OF mindfulness, circle your responses to the following questions, which reflect some common barriers or blocks to mindfulness.

BARRIERS TO MINDFULNESS

1. Do I suffer from "hurry sickness"?   YES or NO
   This is a societal tendency to feel rushed and harried even when it is not necessary.

2. Do I measure happiness by future gains and events?   YES or NO
   Evidence of this includes a preoccupation with thoughts such as, "I'll be happy when . . . " "If only . . . "

3. Do I constantly compare the present to the past?   YES or NO
   This is the result of difficulty in letting go of experiences from the past, such as youth, summer, relationships, and so on.

4. Do I normally try to deny or push
away pain?   YES or NO
> *This is indicative of an unwillingness to confront
> the negative in your life.*

5. Do I have unfinished business in my life?   YES or NO
> *This relates to unexpressed feelings for significant
> people in your life and/or unfulfilled tasks or goals.*

6. Am I often bored with routines and normal
day-to-day living?   YES or NO
> *Does life seem dull, and do you often find yourself
> saying, "Another day of the same old thing"?*

7. Am I preoccupied with expectations
about the future?   YES or NO

8. Do I robotically live my life by going through
the same routine day after day without thinking
of the options?   YES or NO

9. Does my life seem to be directed by old
patterns or behaviors from the past?   YES or NO
> *These are old messages and behaviors you learned from fam-
> ily and society about how you should live your life.*

Your responses to these questions provide an indication
of your tendency to be mindful. Obviously there is no perfect

answer, and many personal circumstances may dictate different responses. If you responded yes to most of these questions, you may not be living as mindfully as you could.

Becoming aware of your blocks and barriers to mindfulness offers you the freedom to enjoy this moment. For example, early in my life, I was often guided by a parental message to hurry up. Like many children, I was strongly encouraged to do things quickly. "Hurry and get into the car," "Hurry up or we'll be late," "Hurry with your homework so you can go out and play." Seldom are children or adults praised for moving slowly and deliberately. So naturally I learned to rush through my life.

Reflections

*The past is to be learned from and not lived in, and
the future is to be planned for, not paralyzed by, and
the present is to be enjoyed right now.*
—ANONYMOUS

*For tomorrow I offer no answers, for yesterday I hold
no apologies. This moment is a gift which I honor by
fully living in it.*
—MARY ANNE RADMACHER-HERSHEY

*We live in a "state of internal wanting"—
return to the experience at the moment as it
was for the first time.*
—ROBERT FROST

- Reflect on how often your model of the past does not work for you in the present.

- What painful things do you refuse to look at in your life today?

- What is robbing you of a sense of peace today?

- What expectations for the future are you willing to give up for happiness now?

The Process

The purpose of the technique is not to lock into the breath, but to use the breath as a means of tuning to the present.
—STEPHEN LEVINE

When we are capable of stopping, we begin to see.
—THICH NHAT HANH

Awareness in itself is healing.
—FRITZ PEARLS

Zen comes from an approach to each situation. Each play, each moment is like a breath and a release.
—PHIL JACKSON

IN PART TWO, YOU WILL

- Develop a technique of mindful breathing

- Learn a process for observing the mind and body

- Experience the mindfulness process

MINDFUL BREATHING

I HAVE HAD SEVERAL OPPORTU-nities to spend time in France at the Plum Village Retreat Center, which is also the residence of the Buddhist author and teacher Thich Nhat Hanh. At the entrance to the village, you are greeted by a large sign reading "You have arrived. Enjoy breathing." In this peaceful community mindfulness is practiced twenty-four hours a day with a focus on breathing at the heart of the practice. Any time a bell rings, including the telephone, people all over the village stop, pause, and then bring their awareness back to the breath.

Mindfulness training begins with a focus on breathing. Mindful breathing can offer us physical and mental equilibrium as well as inner harmony. Breathing is a mediator between the body and the mind, connecting the conscious and unconscious.

Most people breathe 17,000 to 24,000 breaths per day, yet few of us are aware of even one of those breathing cycles. Every moment our breath can create balance within us and bring us back to the present. Everything in nature rises, falls, and exists. In the same way, inhalation is a rising, exhalation a falling, and the pause in between is the existing. We can learn to use our breathing as a metaphor for life and the balance that exists in all of nature.

Many individuals have developed poor breathing habits. Males are often told not to cry or to feel emotions; consequently, their feelings are often blocked, and their breathing is impaired. Both men and women are told that to look good, they should stand with their stomach in and their chest out. Once again, proper breathing is impaired. Babies breathe naturally (abdominally). Watch a baby breathe. They are not concerned with how they look. The only time they switch to chest breathing is when they are hungry or feeling discomfort. Likewise, as you become aware of your breathing, you will naturally slow down your breathing patterns and breathe more abdominally or diaphragmatically.

Becoming mindful of breathing provides many benefits. First, the breath becomes a reminder to come back to the present moment. Often you will literally pause as you catch your breath during a moment of activity or excitement. In such a moment, simply observe your breathing and notice how this practice immediately offers a moment to center yourself and literally refocus mind, body, and spirit. One derivation of the word *respiration* is to "re-spirit." Using your breath to center and re-spirit yourself is the core of mindfulness practice.

Breathing also offers you a moment of rest and renewal. Within each breathing cycle is an opportunity to relax, especially during the exhalation phase of the breath. Notice that as you inhale, you become more energized, and as you exhale, you become more relaxed. During periods of lethargy and sleepiness, awareness of the inhalation of the breath will provide the oxygen needed to restore the body. It can be more helpful than a caffeinated drink. In addition, during times of high stress such as work pressures, traffic jams, and relationship difficulties, an awareness of the exhalation or relaxation phase of the breath can bring your body back into balance.

Finally, breathing offers one of the best ways to quiet the mind. A focus on breathing takes your attention away from your preoccupations. As William James said, "The greatest weapon against stress is our ability to choose one thought over another." In this moment as you bring your full awareness to your breathing, you probably are not thinking about other concerns.

MINDFUL BREATHING PRACTICE

1. Find a comfortable sitting position, with your back straight. Relax your hands and arms, or place them in your lap. Once you have learned this exercise, you may choose to keep your eyes either open or closed.

2. Bring your awareness to your breath. Do not change your breathing, but simply observe and experience the in and out of your breath at your nose or the rising and falling of your diaphragm. Connect the in-breath to the out-breath, the out-breath to the in-breath.

Note: To help you stay focused on the breath, repeat phrases and/or words. For example, as you breathe in and out you might repeat phrases such as:

> *Breathing in, I know that I am breathing in.*
> *Breathing out, I know that I am breathing out.*
> OR
> *Breathing in, I calm my body.*
> *Breathing out, I smile.*

Or you may simply repeat a single word after each inhalation and exhalation, such as "in," "out," "calm," or "smile." Creating your own phrases or words may give more meaning to your practice. Thich Nhat Hanh offers many suggestions in his book *The Blooming of a Lotus.*

3. As you breathe, you will naturally become aware of thoughts, feelings, senses, and bodily sensations. As you do, simply note them and then bring your attention back to your breath.

Learning to become aware of and observe your breathing is one of the best ways to learn mindfulness. As you will discover, an awareness of the breath makes it easier to focus on the moment, restore yourself, and quiet the mind. Discover for yourself the positive influence that breathing has on your own sense of balance and control. The Latin word for breath is *spiritus.* Allow the breath to flow through you as a sense of spirit flows through your body.

In many parts of Asia, when temple bells ring, people stop and pause. In many Christian communities the ringing of church bells often reminds the listeners to pause, pray, and reflect. One of the best ways to practice mindful breathing is to stop and pause during the day to break the cycle of "doing," "going," and frenetic activity. After attending my first retreat at Plum Village, I purchased a small bell for the family household. The bell sits in a prominent location ready to be rung by anyone passing by. The sound of the bell is then a reminder to each person in the house to stop, pause, and take a deep slow breath. On a recent family vacation, our young niece and nephew quickly discovered the bell and its purpose. When the activity level became too hectic, Christopher or Elise would often ring the bell, breathe, and then smile at the sudden pleasure they felt in slowing down (and getting the adults to do so as well!). We had discovered a tiny but wonderful way to teach little children about peace as well as mindfulness.

Reflections

Life starts with a breath and ends with a breath.
—YOGI BHAJAN

Our breath is the bridge from our body to our mind.
—THICH NHAT HANH

Watch breath, soften belly, open heart, has become a wake-up call for mindfulness and mercy, which takes people beyond the mind-body of suffering into the deep peace of their healing.
—STEPHEN LEVINE

- Identify a time or times in which you will be able to practice mindful breathing on a daily basis.

- In what situations in your personal world might you use breathing to come back to the present moment, to renew yourself, and to quiet your mind?

- How might you use bells in your life to remind you and your family to pause, breathe, and enjoy the moment?

MINDFULNESS
PROCESS

A FAMOUS MEDITATION TEACHER was once asked, "How long do you meditate each day?" The reply was, "Formally, for several hours per day I sit and meditate, and informally I meditate all day long, with every activity becoming the focus of my meditation." St. Paul, a Christian saint, was once asked how long he prayed every day. His reply was similar: "I pray for several hours a day, however, I hope my life is a prayer." Learning to become more mindful is not about creating a constantly blissful state. It is about being present in every activity and every relationship. It is the process of being awake to life.

The practice of mindfulness is often sabotaged by various interruptions and distractions. For example, how many times in your workday do you find yourself thinking about the upcoming weekend? Or how many times are you relaxing on the weekend while preoccupied with thoughts of work? The mind naturally pays attention to thoughts, feelings, sensations, and experiences. Thoughts often provoke worry about the past and anxiety about the future. Feelings may arise that are pleasant, unpleasant, or neutral. The senses are constantly providing stimuli through our sight, hearing, taste, smell, and touch. Finally, our bodies are in a state of constant physiological change, involving such things as muscular tension, breathing rate, comfort, and pain.

To best learn about mindfulness, begin by finding a comfortable place to sit where you will be free of distractions for whatever period of time you have available. Start with the mindful breathing process. With your awareness focused on the in and out of your breath, begin—without judgment and with patience—to explore your thoughts, senses, feelings, and bodily experiences as if you were a beginner attempting to learn more about yourself.

Thoughts. What am I thinking now? What kind of thoughts are most frequent? Count thoughts as if you were counting trees, sheep, or money. Note the beginning of a thought, its middle, and then follow the thought to its end. Thoughts and small children have one thing in common: they need attention! Recognize what happens to your thoughts as you simply notice and label each one as "thinking," and then return to your breath.

Sensing. Life is an accumulation of the sensory experiences that we have moment by moment. Our ability to become aware of our senses is one of the most basic ways to experience life fully. Seeing, hearing, tasting, smelling, and touching make up the primary senses. Look around you. What are you *seeing*? Notice every sound from within your body and in your surroundings. What are you *hearing*? What are you *smelling* at this moment? "Braille" (touch) your immediate environment. What are you experiencing while *touching*? Slowly eat a favorite food. What do you notice as you are *tasting*? Continue to notice and label *what* you are sensing and *how* you are sensing it (for example, label the sound of wind "hearing," or the sight of a beautiful flower "seeing"). Notice and label what you are sensing at this moment, experience the sensation fully, and then return to your breath.

Feeling. Thoughts and sensations create within us a variety of feelings that are pleasant, unpleasant, or neutral. Pleasant feelings, such as joy, gratitude, and peacefulness, often enhance the mindfulness process. It is easy to be present for exciting and happy moments. Unpleasant feelings, such as anger and sadness, are most often avoided. Neutral feelings are typical during times of boredom or periods during which nothing pleasant or unpleasant arises. Notice what you are feeling at this moment. Are your feelings pleasant, unpleasant, or neutral? What specific feelings are you experiencing? Notice and label what you are feeling at this moment, experience the sensation fully, and return to your breath.

Bodily experiences. Every moment lived in awareness offers information regarding changes going on within your body. Note for a moment how your breathing changes. Recognize areas of discomfort or pain, most often reflected in muscular tension. Become aware of any temperature shifts between warmth and coolness in various parts of your body. What are you experiencing in your body at this moment? Notice and label what you are experiencing in this moment (for example, label tightness in the neck and shoulders as "tension"), experience the sensation fully, and return to your breath.

As you gradually become more aware of your thoughts, feelings, sensations, and bodily experiences, you are literally "coming to your senses" and enhancing your potential for becoming more mindful.

As simple and beautiful as the process may be, mindfulness requires time each day for daily practice. First, begin by focusing on your breathing as described earlier. During daily practice sessions, keep in mind that your purpose is to focus on your breath. Eventually, you can learn to apply mindfulness to nearly every moment of your life. To practice and enhance mindfulness in daily life, consider the following process:

1. What is your purpose in this moment?

(For example, during your daily practice, use focusing on your breath as your purpose. Other purposes you may use include such activities as completing a report, talking to a patient/client, or reading a bedtime story to your child.)

What am I here for? Returning to your purpose in the moment offers a focus for your practice.

2. When your mind wanders, stop and observe: at this moment, where is my awareness or attention?

What am I thinking? (about the past or future, planning, worrying)

What am I feeling? (pleasant, unpleasant, neutral)

What am I sensing? (seeing, hearing, tasting, smelling, touching)

What am I experiencing in my body? (tension, breath, tightness)

Simply note thinking, feeling, sensing, or whatever you are experiencing in your body.

3. Bring your awareness/attention back to the moment and your purpose by breathing in and breathing out.
Do not attempt to change your breathing, but merely observe and experience the in-and-out of your breath and return to your purpose in the moment.

4. Repeat these steps as necessary to bring yourself back to the moment.

FINDING A QUIET PLACE and consistent time each day to practice helps develop this process, which can slowly be applied to all activities, experiences, and interactions. Life is filled with many distractions, and the process of mindfulness is about simply learning to become aware of what you are thinking, sensing, feeling, and experiencing and returning to the present moment. It's all about coming back, returning to *now*.

Reflections

*If mindfulness refers to keeping one's consciousness
alive to the present reality, then one must practice
right now in one's daily life, not only during
meditation sessions.*

—THICH NHAT HANH

*Mindfulness is the practice of aiming your attention,
moment by moment, in the direction of your purpose.
It is called mindfulness, because you have to keep your
purpose in mind as you watch your attention. Then,
whenever you notice that your aim has drifted off
purpose, you calmly realign it.*

—FRANK ANDREWS

*It is good to have an end to journey toward;
but it is the journey that matters in the end.*

—URSULA K. LEGUIN

- Explore ways in which awareness might be helpful in healing yourself and your relationships.

- In what circumstances, both personally and professionally, might you apply the mindfulness process to your life?

PART THREE

Applications of Mindfulness

If you are at all successful in developing this type of detached witnessing (it does take time), you will be able to look upon the events occurring in your mind-and-body with the very same impartiality that you would look upon clouds floating through the sky, water rushing in a stream, rain cascading on a roof, or any other objects in your field of awareness.

—KEN WILBER

Life is filled with suffering, but it is also filled with many wonders, like the blue sky, the sunshine, the eyes of a baby. To suffer is not enough. We must also be in touch with the wonders of life. They are within us and all around us, everywhere, any time.

—THICH NHAT HANH

Don't look to the past in anger nor the future in fear, but around in awareness.

—JAMES THURBER

IN PART THREE, YOU WILL

- Manage stress

- Quiet the mind

- Transform difficult feelings

- Enhance concentration and productivity

- Deepen relationships

- Learn to complete unfinished business

- Experience daily activities mindfully

MANAGING
STRESS

THERE IS A STORY OF A farmer and his son who worked their small farm with the help of one horse. One day the horse ran away, and all the neighbors sympathetically said, "Such bad luck!" The farmer replied, "Bad luck, good luck." A short time later the lost horse returned to his stable and brought with him four wild mares. "What wonderful luck!" the neighbors now said. "Good luck, bad luck, who knows?" replied the farmer. Several weeks later the son, in training one of the wild horses, fell and broke his leg. "Bad luck, good luck," voiced his dad. Shortly thereafter, the military arrived to recruit all able young men for the service. Since the farmer's son had broken his leg, he was of no use to the military. "Bad luck or good luck?" It depends on your interpretation of the experience!

Stress is a normal psycho/physiological response to events in our life. This response is innate and is often a means of self-preservation. Conversely, *distress* is often the result of our *interpretation* of the events in our life. Epictetus, a first-century Roman philosopher, makes this clear with his statement, "Man is not disturbed by events, but by the view he takes of them." Thus, any event in our life can be labeled as stress or distress based upon our interpretation or, even more significantly, our judgment of the particular event.

The psychologist Ken Wilber has written, "If we can watch or witness our distress, we prove ourselves thereby to be 'distress-less,' free of the witnessed turmoil." Exploring that process may provide an understanding of how both mindfulness and becoming acquainted with the "witness" within you can help reduce the potential negative psychological and physical impact of events in your life.

Distress begins with a simple thought, but years later it may become a piece of unfinished business that reduces our potential for experiencing peace, joy, and happiness. The anatomy of distress essentially unfolds as follows:

1. **Awareness/consciousness** occurs when you see, hear, smell, taste, experience, and/or think in response to a recollection or a direct contact with some object, person, activity, and/or environment.

> Example: as you enjoy your gardening, you become aware of— conscious of—a project at work.

2. **Feelings then arise that are pleasant, unpleasant, and/or neutral.**

> Example: the thought of the project is unpleasant.

3. **Perceptions and reasoning begins to occur.** Most often, an evaluation or judgment is made.

> Example: this project is unpleasant, difficult, and you think you should be putting in extra time now, instead of gardening.

4. Distorted and exaggerated thinking often follows the judgment or evaluation. This kind of thinking most often has roots in *wants*, *desires*, our *concept or perception of self*, and the *views and opinions* (models) we often attach to one way of thinking, being, or doing.

> Example: You think, "What's wrong with me? Why is this project so hard for me and not for Joe? I shouldn't be enjoying gardening when I have more important things to do."

5. Distorted and/or exaggerated thinking continues. Now you become focused or "caught" on the problem, and this often creates distress because you continue to attach various judgmental thoughts, feelings, and bodily sensations to the experience. This is usually enhanced by the number of "shoulds" and "ought-tos" you attach to the experience!

> Example: Your preoccupation with the problem continues all weekend. You worry constantly, have trouble sleeping, and feel bad. Based on this exaggerated thinking, you have been negatively affected both mentally and physically.

Exploring this model can help us to understand how a simple thought can create suffering and distress. Learning to become mindful or simply to witness the scenario as it unfolds can be a powerful way of changing potentially distressful situations. For example, by becoming mindful at the very moment in which unpleasant thoughts arise (the project at work, for example), you can simply note and/or witness the thought ("Hmm . . . a work thought") before exaggerated thinking or judgments become the focal point of your awareness. By applying the mindfulness practice to any stressful situation, you learn to *witness* rather than react.

Several years ago, my wife and I had planned a ten-day vacation on the Garden Island of Kauai, Hawaii. For months we reviewed the brochures, talked with travel agents and friends who had vacationed there before. Daily we talked about our trip—time to walk on the beach, rounds of golf, snorkeling, and the whale watching trips. Soon the big day arrived and we flew to sunny Hawaii. Upon arrival we were greeted by torrential rains, which we thought would be temporary. Day after day the rain continued and our outlook dimmed. All the things we had planned to do for months were canceled day by day as the storm continued. The model that we created in our minds about our trip to Hawaii was not to be. In our preoccupation with what we wanted to experience, we missed really experiencing the island in the rain and, also, I suspect, many wonderful relaxing moments. We discovered that our models and expectations for the experience created unnecessary stress for both of us. Learning to truly witness and not become attached to wants, desires, views, and opinions allows us to be free to make choices and create new and exciting experiences.

You may be familiar with accounts of individuals who have had a near-death or out-of-body experience. These individuals often witness their trauma and the accompanying resuscitation attempts from unusual and unique vantage points, without feeling or attachment to the event. You need not have a near-death or out-of-body experience to also become a witness to events in your life!

Reflections

Pain is inevitable; suffering is optional.
—ANONYMOUS

In the face of suffering,
one has no right to turn away, not to see.
—ELIE WIESEL

Thus, ultimately to try to escape a distress merely
perpetuates that distress. What is so upsetting is
not the distress itself, but our attachment to that
distress. We identify with it, and that alone is
the real difficulty.
—KEN WILBER

- When you find yourself involved in a stressful situation, begin to witness the in-and-out of your breath. Stop and observe: in this moment, where is my awareness or attention? Witness and label your thinking, feeling, sensing, and bodily experiences. Bring your awareness/attention back to the moment by breathing in and out. The key is to witness what is causing the distress. By simply becoming an impartial observer, separate and unattached, you soon realize that the distress is simply caused by thoughts, feelings, senses, or bodily experiences. In learning to witness, you begin to see yourself as an outside observer. The next time you have a headache, for example, try the witnessing process to help detach yourself not only from the pain, but, perhaps, the source of the pain as well.

- Explore situations in your life that you cannot change. Obviously, it is hard to change other people. How can you learn to witness situations you cannot change rather than react to them?

QUIETING
THE
MIND

MANY PEOPLE FEEL UNCOM-fortable when it is quiet. They seem more comfortable when the television is on, the radio is playing, or when they are busy with activities. I often ask people, "What is the one way you quiet your mind?" Their responses are varied and usually include activities such as music, exercise, watching movies, and reading—all activities which can be pleasurable and relaxing and can *also* be a form of distraction or diversion. Sometimes if we fill our time with activity, we do not have to experience what is really going on in our lives. I have always felt that the deepest form of therapy for me is to attend a meditation retreat. During these retreats and after several days of silence, I would often discover things about myself that I never recognized before. It is very common during long periods of silence to have people begin to cry and face issues from the past that have clouded their ability to be present. Two major sources of stress are the mind and the way in which we interpret every situation in our lives. Our bodies respond physiologically to the thoughts that we hang on to (past or future thinking) or that result from distorted thinking. Most people are troubled with such thoughts at bedtime or in the middle of the night. Insomnia is a common complaint often aggravated by distorted thinking and a preoccupation with the past or future.

Living in the present is difficult when you have a lot on your mind. Most stress originates from your thoughts of the past or concerns about the future. How many times have you become preoccupied with the potential disasters of some event in the future, only to realize when the time finally arrived that most of your worrying was in vain?

Clearly, it is important to plan for the future, but not to be obsessed with its outcome. In planning, it is human nature to consider all possible negative consequences, or the so-called "worst-case scenario." However, according to cognitive therapists, the mind has a tendency to create distortions, referred to as cognitive distortions or distorted thinking. All these distortions and preoccupations with the past or the future become invitations to live outside the present moment. But more significantly, these thoughts become the basis for stress and anxiety. Learning to quiet the mind is the basis for becoming more mindful and open to the beauty surrounding us.

There are many techniques for quieting the mind. Most techniques focus on a word, phrase, sound, or an object such as the flame of a candle to help you become more focused and centered. The following technique to quiet the mind is similar to the basic mindfulness process with emphasis placed on labeling *thoughts*. This strategy may be helpful for those who have difficulty falling asleep or at any time when one is preoccupied with certain thoughts.

QUIETING THE MIND: BASIC PRACTICE

SINCE MOST DISTRESS RELATES to a preoccupation with thoughts, practice observing these thoughts and then letting go of them.

1. Begin to focus on your breath at the tip of your nostrils or on the rising and falling of the abdomen. Keep your attention on the breath.

2. Naturally, thoughts will enter your consciousness. Use your thoughts as the object of relaxation or meditation. As thoughts arise in your mind, simply become aware of them and note the general nature of your thinking, or label the thought as one of hunger, pain, sleep, or sex, for example.

3. Bring your attention back to your breath. Through a simple awareness of the thought, it loses some of its power. Do not resist the thought, since what you resist persists. Stress and tension develop as we become preoccupied with certain thoughts.

When the mind is quiet the body is quiet. When the body is quiet the mind is quiet. Learning to quiet your mind is one of the most basic ways to become relaxed and peaceful.

Reflections

Worrying about the future is like trying to eat the hole in a doughnut. It's munching on what isn't.
—BARRY NEIL KAUFMAN

Unlike achieving things worth having, to achieve things worth being usually requires long periods of solitude.
—MEYER FRIEDMAN AND RAY ROSENMAN

The trouble with Archie is he don't know how to worry without getting upset.
—EDITH BUNKER (ON HER SITCOM HUSBAND, ARCHIE BUNKER)

The fact that the mind rules the body is, in spite of its neglect by biology and medicine, the most fundamental fact which we know about the process of life.
—FRANZ ALEXANDER, M.D.

Man is disturbed not by things, but by his opinion of things.
—EPICTETUS, FIRST-CENTURY ROMAN PHILOSOPHER

- Can you identify situations in which you can use the "quieting the mind" technique? For example, the technique was helpful to me at several times while writing this book. I discovered that my thoughts about getting my work to the editor would get in the way of clarifying a point or staying with the theme of the present chapter. By taking a moment to label my thoughts ("hurry thought") and then breathe, I could quickly bring myself back to the task at hand.

- Using a "beginner's mind," take some time to explore the nature of your thoughts. Note the beginning and ending of each thought, recognize the types of thoughts you are experiencing, and witness how thoughts are only thoughts.

TRANSFORMING
FEELINGS

S TRESS IS OFTEN CREATED when we are preoccupied with thoughts and feelings. Feelings in particular can create a vicious cycle of thinking that leads to pleasant, unpleasant, and neutral states. There are many ways to cope with feelings, such as physical activity and talking or debriefing with others. However, mindfulness can also help us cope with or transform our feelings.

TRANSFORMING FEELINGS:
BASIC PRACTICE

TO TRANSFORM A FEELING, begin with mindful breathing. Focus on your breath at the tip of your nostrils or the abdomen. Keep your attention on the breath flowing in and out. Naturally, thoughts will enter your consciousness and may lead to a feeling state, such as anger. As that feeling enters your consciousness, simply become aware of it, and then bring your attention back to your breath. Through a simple awareness of the feeling, it loses some of its power. In this moment accept the feeling. Do not resist. Embrace it.

Befriend the anger and become one with it. As you breathe in and breathe out, observe and study the anger. Begin to calm the anger through your mindful breathing and the repetition of verses, such as this phrase used at the Plum Village Retreat Center:

Experiencing the feeling of anger in me, I breathe in.
Smiling at the feeling of anger in me, I breathe out.

Preferably, create your own short phrases, and repeat and connect them with each breathing cycle. Here are some examples:

Breathing in, I recognize my anger.
Breathing out, I am aware of how angry I am.
Breathing in, I see my anger overwhelming me.
Breathing out, I recognize that the anger affects my
entire body.

Through continued awareness and a sense of calmness, you will find it becomes easier to change the intensity of the anger and gradually release the anger, letting it go.

Many times I have used walking as a means of becoming aware of and transforming a feeling. Simply apply the same verses while walking. Coordinate your steps to the phrase "Breathing in and stepping, I experience my anger. Breathing out and stepping, I feel the anger overwhelm me." The key is to personalize the phrases so that you allow yourself to experience the feeling rather than resist it. After a short walk, I find that the feeling has lost its intensity and I feel renewed both emotionally *and* physically.

If the feeling state is not strong, simply note the feeling and then return your focus to your breath. Through your awareness of the feeling, the intensity of the feeling will change in the same way that nature is constantly changing.

Reflections

You cannot perceive beauty but with a serene mind.
—HENRY DAVID THOREAU

I don't express anger,
I get a tumor instead.
—WOODY ALLEN

The only way out is through.
—ROBERT FROST

In order to have real transformation,
we have to deal with the roots of our anger.
If we don't, the seeds of anger will grow again.
—THICH NHAT HANH

- Think of one feeling that you typically have difficulty with; then allow yourself some time to practice the basic technique for transforming feelings described in this chapter. After completing this practice session, take some time to write about your experience. Note how you are feeling in this moment.

- In what way do you resist feelings as they arise? Keeping busy, watching television, or having music on are several examples.

ENHANCING CONCENTRATION AND PRODUCTIVITY

As a reformed "Type A" personality (coronary prone individuals who are always in a hurry in their attempt to feel in control), I have continually struggled with concentrating and staying focused. My underlying desire to hurry together with my tendency to think "it can wait" did not help matters. I would compensate with hurrying even more and then spending more time than was necessary on personal and professional assignments, jobs, and projects. As I began to practice mindfulness, I found to my surprise that I was able to stay focused longer, and gradually I could work more effectively and successfully.

As you learn the practice of mindfulness and focus on breathing, your quality of concentration will also improve. Studies of experienced meditators indicate an ability to stay focused for long periods of time. As you practice mindfulness, you will find that your greatest distractions result from constant thoughts, feelings, and sensations. Soon you learn to quickly become aware of and witness the distractions. For example, as I write this book, I am often distracted by thoughts and feelings, such as "take a break" or "I don't like doing this now." If I react to every distraction, it is clear that I will accomplish very little.

In addition to your ongoing mindfulness practice, applying the basic mindfulness process to work projects is an effective way to enhance your productivity. Remember:

Step 1: What is my purpose in this moment?

> Example: to complete this memo announcing tomorrow's meeting.

Step 2: When your mind wanders, stop and observe: What am I thinking, feeling, sensing, or experiencing?

> Example: in the process of completing this memo, I am reminded of going home in the rush-hour traffic.

Step 3: Simply note your thought, breathe, and bring your attention back to the project.

> Example: instead of being preoccupied with the traffic, I simply note my thoughts regarding the traffic and use my breath as a reminder to concentrate on completing the memo.

Here are some other strategies for enhancing your productivity and concentration:

1. Have a clear purpose and/or goal(s) for the work at hand.

2. Bracket time for each project. Being clear on the amount of time that you have available for each project will add structure to your work. Often when I know that I have thirty

minutes to complete a task, I am more likely to stay focused and complete the job in the allotted time.

3. Begin tasks you have a chance of completing. Not only does this help you stay focused, but it also offers the intrinsic rewards found in completion. If the project is multifaceted, divide it by setting mini-goals along the way, and complete each of these in the allotted time.

4. Take time along the way to offer feedback to yourself or others who are working with you on the project. Look at the tree you trimmed or the memo you just wrote, and admire and validate yourself for completing the tasks. In working with others, remember their need for feedback, too.

Reflections

If you pay attention at every moment, you form a new relationship to time. In some magical way, by slowing down, you become more efficient, productive, and energetic, focusing without distraction directly on the task in front of you. Not only do you become immersed in the moment, you become that moment.

—MICHAEL RAY

The first landmark in concentration comes when the meditator's mind is unaffected both by outer distractions, such as nearby sounds, and by the turbulence of his own assorted thoughts and feelings.

—DANIEL GOLEMAN

- Make a list of the most important activities you need to complete each day to be successful. Now visualize yourself being mindful during the completion of each activity. Close your eyes and see yourself entering into a state of mindfulness as you undertake and complete the most important projects.

- Learn to bracket your work or activities. When you have a project to do, set a timer for thirty minutes and focus on only that activity. When you get distracted, note the distraction and continue to focus on the task at hand.

DEEPENING
RELATIONSHIPS

GEORGE BERNARD SHAW once said, "My tailor is the wisest of persons who comes to see me. Every time he comes to see me, he takes new measurements." How do you enter each interaction in your relationships? Are you like the tailor, who looks at each person as if he were seeing that person for the first time? Or do you take other people for granted because you have previous experience with them and have already sized them up? Do you ever consider that they may have changed or grown since your last interaction? How often are you truly present with others?

I recall a favorite story from a workshop participant about children and being present. He was baby-sitting his granddaughter, and after playing several games with her he decided to take a break and read the paper with the television on. After several minutes during which her questions to her grandfather went unanswered, she took the paper her grandpa was reading and began to shake it while saying, "Grandpa, look at me with your eyes." Children really know when we are not *with* them!

In both a personal and a professional sense, the greatest gift we give to one another is our presence. In my work with caregivers, I have realized that one of the most powerful ingredients for enhancing healing and change is presence. Carl Rogers, the father of humanistic psychology, was known for his emotional presence and openness. Clients and colleagues often remarked that his eyes were really seeing them, and his ears were fully taking in their words. In thinking of the people that I enjoy being with, I recognize that the quality that I admire most is their presence, or their willingness to convey to me that in this moment no one else is more important.

Learning to listen to another person becomes the best strategy for enhancing presence. Author Chogyam Trungpa identifies three kinds of listening that are often destructive to meaningful relationships. In the first kind of listening, your mind is wandering so much that there is no room at all for anything that's being said—you are just there physically. In the second kind, your mind is relating somewhat to what's being said, but basically it is still wandering. In the third kind, your mind is filled with such emotions as judgment, negativity, and resentment. You have mixed emotions about what is being said and are unable to really *hear* another. Can you relate to any of these examples? Learning to be present for another requires an ability to let go of thoughts that block true intimacy with another human being. In addition, learning to listen requires the constant application of the basic mindfulness process discussed earlier in this book. Remember:

Step 1: My purpose at this moment is to be with this person. I use this person as the source of meditation, meaning that I "attend to" him or her.

Step 2: When my presence is distracted, I note the distraction as thinking, feeling, sensing, or experiencing.

Step 3: I become aware of my breathing and bring my attention back to the person.

Repeat these steps whenever you are distracted. The most important person to be with is the person you are with. This ongoing technique lets us provide the best gift we have—our complete self—to each person.

IN LOOKING BACK at an earlier time in my life, I can now painfully recall many moments when I was physically present with others and not really there. As a young parent, I was the kind of dad who would skip pages while reading bedtime stories to my son and daughter. Always in a hurry to get to the next moment and get the children to bed, I missed many opportunities to really be there for those I loved. After sharing this in my workshops and classes, many of the participants laughed because they too could relate to missing quality time with the important people in their lives.

Love is the essence and foundation of all relationships. Healthy relationships are best enhanced when one demonstrates a strong love and compassion for self. The saying, "Love thy neighbor as thyself" infers equality. Without caring for ourselves, it is difficult to care for others. A nurse at a recent conference reflected on the importance of self-care in her work. Her favorite saying was "I can't do you if I don't do me."

One way to enhance your relationships is to practice loving kindness to yourself and others. According to Sharon Salzberg, in her book *Loving Kindness: The Revolutionary Art of Happiness*, there are classically four phrases of loving kindness:

"May *I* be free from danger."
"May *I* have mental happiness."
"May *I* have physical happiness."
"May *I* have ease of well-being."

In practicing these phrases, bring your awareness to your breath and begin mindful breathing. Coordinate the phrases to each breath and begin to nourish yourself with these simple statements. After a short time of repeating these phrases to yourself, think of a relationship that is important to you. See that person in your mind's eye and begin to say the same statements with their well-being in mind:

"May *you* be free from danger."
"May *you* have mental happiness."
"May *you* have physical happiness."
"May *you* have ease of well-being."

In this process you can shift the benefactor of your kind thoughts to any person that you know from the past and in the present, and especially to those individuals with whom your relationship has been or currently is painful. In repeating these phrases, you are learning to heal yourself and deepen your relationships with others.

Reflections

Every time we meet is the first time, because every time you are different, as I also am. We do not step twice in the same river, said Heraclitus; this was said very truly, as the river flows without end, and its waters are never the same.

—CARLOS VALLES

Making contact involves two people at a time and three parts.
Each person in contact with himself or herself and each in contact with the other.

—VIRGINIA SATIR

To be truly present with another person, I must find what interests me, what distracts me from my busy inner world, which is flooded with chatter and images.

—DON HANLON JOHNSON

- When we ask others, "What are the traits of individuals you like to be with?" they often mention traits and qualities associated with mindfulness. Create your own list and discover for yourself how mindfulness is often one of the key ingredients we value most in others.

- Think about the most important people in your life. Consider applying this strategy of mindfulness to your next interaction with them. See them as if you were a tailor, noting everything about them in a new and fresh way. Practice this with every person you meet, familiar and unfamiliar. What are the typical distractions that prevent you from truly being with another individual? Use each person as a reminder to be mindful. How can you create more mindful moments with those you love?

COMPLETING
UNFINISHED
BUSINESS

IN THE PROCESS OF QUIETING your mind and becoming more mindful, it is likely that you will become aware of some of your unfinished business. In addition, your efforts to live mindfully may be hampered by this unfinished business, which death and dying specialist Dr. Elisabeth Kübler-Ross defines as "something that is incomplete in our lives that deprives us of a sense of peace." Unfinished business almost always involves relationships and things that have been said or left unsaid, done or not done. It also includes tasks never completed, trips not taken, and dreams and goals not fulfilled. I will always remember a favorite college professor of mine, Don Willie. Professor Willie was one person who believed in me and saw my potential. I often wanted to take time to thank him for his inspiration and support. But my motivation to do so seemed to get lost in busy days and career and family matters. Months turned into years, and one day I read about his death in the alumni newsletter. "Why didn't I thank him? Why didn't I write him a letter or send a card?" "Did he know he made a difference in my life?" This is an example of just one piece of unfinished business. His loss became an important reminder to me that now is the time to express my feelings toward others. Say the I Love You *now*. Send those flowers to a loved one *now*. Appreciate someone *now*. Forgive someone *now*. Completing your unfinished business allows you to let go of the past and live more fully in the present moment. As you examine your life, your goals, your relationships, what is unfinished? What "baggage" from the past do you carry with you day to day? What keeps robbing you of a sense of peace?

Psychologically speaking, all experiences stay with us until we achieve closure with them. Whenever unfinished business forms the center of existence, the mind is hampered. The content of unfinished business and how it is handled are key to living life more fully. How do you know that you have unfinished business? Consider the following questions:

- Are you preoccupied with the thought of a person or a past experience?
- Do you cry easily or get angry at the thought of this person or experience?
- Are your thoughts frequently prefaced by "If only . . ."?
- Do you find yourself becoming emotionally involved with another person's problems when they are similar to your own problems?
- What are you currently putting off in your life?

Sometimes it is helpful to use death as an advisor in these situations. As you ponder what will be your own death one day, what is it that you would regret leaving undone at the end of your life?

Living and interacting with others in the world is bound to create stressful situations in our lives. As we have discussed, many of the problems with others are often based on unfinished business, which may result in hurt feelings and sometimes even more serious problems. Thich Nhat Hanh has developed a strategy for letting go called "Beginning Anew." He suggests that individuals who live together have a weekly meeting, preferably on a day of the week when individual and family pressures are least demanding. Develop a specific time period and as much as possible require that all members of the household be present. Create a pleasant environment and, if possible, have everyone sit in a circle or around the table. An elder member of the group should run the meeting, although this task can be passed around depending on the age of the participants. The following guidelines are suggested:

1. Take a moment to renew yourself by relaxing and talking about the day and slowly begin to become more peaceful by taking a few deep, long breaths.

2. Each person in the group takes a turn and acknowledges each person in the circle in some positive, caring way. The person sharing the compliments has the floor, and the others must just sit and savor the comments. (Some Native American cultures use a "talking stick" to indicate that the person holding the stick is the only one allowed to speak.) All that is required of the other members is to listen and fully experience the positive things being said to them.

3. Next, express any regrets for your shortcomings or anything hurtful that was said or done to another. Use "I" messages such as "**I** was angry when you came in so late the other night. **I** was worried about you." Avoid accusations, blaming, and defensiveness.

4. Allow time for everyone to express their appreciations, individual shortcomings, and resentments or difficulties with others.

5. Conclude with a snack, a walk, or a meal together. By meeting on a weekly or biweekly basis, members of the family or community will have an opportunity to debrief or to let go of the problems and feelings that may build over time and prevent them from living together in harmony. To create peace on our planet, we need to begin with ourselves and those we love.

Note: Sometimes the core of unfinished business is related to early pain and trauma, such as abuse and incest. If your life is continually affected by these experiences, please consider seeking professional assistance.

Reflections

We should live our life like a very hot fire, so there is nothing left behind—everything is burned to a white ash.

—SUZUKI ROSHI

Two monks were walking along a road, and they come to a river.

On the bank was a beautiful young woman who was afraid to cross the river by herself. One of the monks gallantly stepped forth and offered her a ride on his shoulders. Upon reaching the other side, she thanked the monk and they went their separate ways. About one hundred steps down the road, the second monk asked the first, "How could you do that? You are a monk, a renunciate. You should not be carrying beautiful women around on your shoulders." To which the first monk replied, "Oh, are you still carrying her? I let her down when we reached the shore."

—TRADITIONAL ZEN STORY

If you don't finish your unfinished childhood business, your future becomes your past.

—PAUL BRENNER

*Hanging on to resentment is allowing
someone you despise
to live rent free in your head.*
—ANONYMOUS

- If you had only one year to live and could live it in relatively good health, what would you do differently? (How do you know you don't have a year to live?)

- If you knew you would die tomorrow and could make one telephone call, who would you call? What would you say? What unfinished business would be part of your conversation?

DAILY
ACTIVITIES

MINDFULNESS CAN BECOME a part of all our daily activities. The following discourses on mindful eating and walking are just two examples of mindfulness applied to our daily lives.

MINDFUL EATING

WHEN MINDFULNESS IS applied to eating, it becomes a powerful tool that can enhance the joy and beneficial effects of food. Eating is all too frequently a "mindless" activity as we gulp our meals down and combine them with other activities, such as reading the newspaper, watching television, or interacting with the family. Since eating then becomes a secondary experience, its real pleasure is often missed.

MINDFUL EATING PROCESS

1. Before eating, remember your purpose: *to eat.*

2. Before eating, take a moment to become aware of your breathing.

3. Slow down the overall eating process. Chew your food slowly.

4. Involve all of your senses (sight, hearing, taste, smell, touch) in experiencing your meal.

5. As your mind wanders, bring your awareness back to the moment. Eating is the object of your attention.

By becoming mindful, you will find that eating becomes a more pleasing and fulfilling experience. For some people, becoming mindful about their eating process may be one of the best underlying strategies for weight control. Food that is chewed slowly is easily digested, and you are less likely to overeat when you eat in mindful ways.

Think about your last meal. Can you recall the various tastes, smells, and textures that you experienced?

Reflections

To eat mindfully, pay close attention to each bite.
—DANIEL GOLEMAN
AND TARA BENNETT-GOLEMAN

What is the use of planning to be able to eat next week, unless I can really enjoy the meals when they come? If I am so busy planning how to eat next week that I cannot fully enjoy what I am eating now, I will be in the same predicament when next week's meals become now.
—ALAN WATTS

We develop this sense of interconnectedness by acknowledging all that is eaten in its original form: envisioning the wheat that comprises the bread, the milk of the cow, the pod of the pea. The ocean of fish. And the sun which feeds them all.
We take in the sacred, the germ of life, like the Eucharist, in gratitude and respect.
—STEPHEN LEVINE

When was the last time you had a glass of water and really drank it?
—THOMAS MERTON

MINDFUL WALKING

TO WALK MINDFULLY is to meditate while you walk. Think how much time you spend walking on a daily basis. Typically, the purpose of your walking is to go somewhere, to arrive. Because of "hurry sickness" or a lack of awareness, we often miss the real journey. Recalling hikes and walks I've taken in the past, I believe my main purpose was always to arrive somewhere, and when I was walking with another person, I wanted to arrive first! Learning to walk mindfully is not as easy as it seems. The purpose of learning to walk mindfully is to walk and enjoy the walking itself. That means learning to focus on the *walking* and **not** on the *destination*.

MINDFUL WALKING PROCESS

1. Recall your purpose in this moment: *to walk.*

2. Stop and observe: where is my awareness or attention?

3. Become aware of your breathing. Focus on the in-breath and the out-breath.

4. Begin walking with your left foot, and while breathing in say, "In." As your right foot moves forward, breathe out and say, "Out." Vary your pace and breathing to suit your needs and the environment.

5. As your mind wanders, bring your awareness/attention back to the moment by breathing in and breathing out as you walk.

Note: When walking indoors, your pace will be slower, usually one or two steps for each in-breath and the same for each out-breath. Outdoors, coordinate your breathing with your steps. You may find that three or four steps per in-breath and out-breath may be suitable for you. Using the words, "In, in, in, out, out, out," can help you to stay focused.

HAVING READ THIS section and perhaps even tried some mindful walking, you may think that this process can be rather tedious or frustrating. Think about what you may experience along the journey that you previously have missed. Flowers, trees, wind, sky, children laughing, raindrops on the pavement, stunning architecture, the smiles of others. A new world opens up to you, and as it does, stop, pause, and enjoy each scene, sound, smell, and experience along the way. Breathe! Continue your focus on walking.

Recently, on a hike with my son to a beautiful mountain peak, we talked all the way to the top. One solid hour of walking and talking. He decided that on the way down we would walk mindfully without talking. Later, reflecting on that hike, we both commented on how we became closer as father and son as we shared thoughts and feelings while we walked up the mountain. We also recognized how many more flowers, birds, and trees we saw or heard on the way down. The journey up the mountain created moments of intimacy between a father and son. The journey down the mountain created intimacy between father, son, mountain, and nature.

Reflections

Each step is life, each step is joy and peace.
—THICH NHAT HANH

It is no use walking anywhere to preach unless our walking is our preaching.
—ST. FRANCIS OF ASSISI

When we walk slowly, the world can fully appear. Not only are the creatures not frightened away by our haste or aggression, but the fine detail of fern and flower, or devastation and disruption become visible.
—JOAN HALIFAX

- Explore ways in which mindfulness is enhanced with every step you take. Consider opportunities for more mindful walking. Use each step as the means of coming back to the present moment. Think about your typical walking patterns. What does your way of walking say about you? If your steps could talk, what would they say?

- Try an experiment in mindful eating using an orange. Take the orange and slowly peel it, smelling the oils that are released from the peel. Do you begin to salivate before you actually taste the orange? Carefully divide the orange into sections, and eat one small piece at a time. What do you notice as the orange touches your lips and tongue? Try this same experiment with a partner whose eyes are closed. Slowly feed the orange to your partner, and notice how all the senses are involved in the process of taste.

PART FOUR

Maintaining a Mindful Lifestyle

The mind should be like a camera loaded with appreciation, ready to capture in full color and in perfect focus the essence of each beautiful moment.
—ANONYMOUS

Make the present moment the best moment of your life.
—THICH NHAT HANH

The only measure of success is this moment, right now. Are we here? If we are here, our practice is perfect.
—DAVID COOPER

IN PART FOUR, YOU WILL

- Learn ways to practice mind-fulness daily

- Develop a process for looking deeply and gaining insight

- Apply mindfulness to your workplace

- Review the meaning and practice of mindfulness

- Develop a personal commit-ment to live more mindfully

DAILY
PRACTICE

BECOMING MINDFUL REQUIRES that you value the importance of the concept, and that you have the discipline to go beyond the reading of this book. Discipline comes from the word *disciple,* which refers to following one's love. In the same way that you cannot plan to become fit by joining a health club and then only attending occasionally, you cannot truly follow this way of being without a plan or program. Mindfulness requires you to exercise the same motivation, discipline, and daily awareness consistently, until it becomes a moment-by-moment practice.

The following suggestions can enhance the practice of mindfulness in your daily life:

1. Set aside some quiet time daily to practice mindful breathing. Create a comfortable space for yourself free of distractions, a "sacred space" just for you. Begin with ten minutes or so of the basic mindfulness practice with the focus on your breath. If time and space permit, mini-sessions throughout the day may be helpful.

2. Find time each day to just be. When I was child, my mother often said, "Gerald, just sit for a while; you are always

on the go!" As adults, so much of our identity centers around our doing. The shoulds and oughts of life often become our guiding force. Consequently, so many adults feel guilty when they are not working, and they will often create additional work for themselves to avoid these guilt feelings. Finding time to do nothing each day is one way to bring balance back into a life filled with doing. Do you have a healthy balance between being and doing? Create a "lazy day" or half-day or a "lazy hour" during which you spend time just being, with no prearranged agenda. If you want to read, read. If you want to sleep, sleep. If you have young children who need tending, arrange with your partner or a friend to be responsible for the children for that time. You can also teach your children to learn to just be by sharing this experience with them.

3. Try to complete personal or professional tasks each day or bracket a certain amount of time for a task such as gardening or grocery shopping so you can be sure it gets done and still have time for you. Apply this same technique to projects at work. For example, my work often involves writing and organizational business planning. If I set aside thirty minutes to write, I will set a timer and write for that time period. As I am interrupted by thoughts, feelings, and such, I note the distraction, breathe, and return to the task at hand.

4. Use mindfulness to enhance relationships. Identify several individuals who are most significant in your life and let them be reminders to be mindful. When you find your mind wandering in conversation, continue to bring your attention back

to the person. Remember, the best gift that you give to each person is your self.

5. Create an environment at home and work that offers opportunities and reminders to be mindful. At home and in the workplace, you can also find reminders to stop, pause, and breathe. A beeper sounds, a phone rings, the buzzer on the microwave goes off, the elevator signals as it opens; all can be used as reminders to take a moment to breathe and then return to the present moment. A bell placed on your desk or the kitchen counter and set to ring randomly provides a reminder to stop, pause, renew. Drive out of your garage, pause, and breathe as you watch the garage door slowly close.

6. Recall the quote, "At any moment, whatever we are experiencing, only one of two things is ever happening: either we are *being* with what is, or else we are *resisting* what is." Think about the kind of things in your life you are resisting right now. Recognize that more psychological energy is used in resisting than in actually doing. During my college days, I had a summer job in a water meter factory. My job was to repetitively test meters for leaks by sending pressurized water through the meter. Looking back, I now realize that I found the job to be a difficult one because of the resistance I had to being there. Had I realized then that by letting go of that resistance, in other words, if I had stopped looking at my watch and mentally complaining, it could have been a much more fulfilling experience for me. How much psychological energy I wasted not wanting to be there!

7. Develop social support for the practice of mindfulness. Practicing mindfulness becomes easier in an office or home when other people are mindful. For example, when I see my wife eating mindfully, I am reminded to focus on the process of eating. In the workplace, when several people begin to exhibit mindful behaviors in their work and interactions, other colleagues are unconsciously and positively affected. Recently, a group of nurses in my workshop decided to use call-bells, beepers, phones, and overhead pages as reminders to briefly pause, breathe, and become more mindful. Through their example, the entire unit soon became a more mindful place to be. Imagine the healing effect that this may have on their interactions and ultimately the health of their patients!

The ultimate goal of daily practice is to create simple reminders that each moment is an opportunity for practicing mindfulness.

Reflections

Are we human beings or human doings?
—ANONYMOUS

You don't get to choose how you're going to die, or when, you can only decide how you're going to live now.
—JOAN BAEZ

IN THE SPACE BELOW make a list of the activities you engage in routinely, such as getting up in the morning, eating breakfast, taking a shower, driving to work, talking to friends, exercising, doing house- or yard work, working, and preparing to go to bed. Be as specific as possible in detailing the activities you engage in on a regular basis. Next to each activity, describe specific ways you will become more mindful during that activity.

EXAMPLE

Regular Activity	Mindful Activity
1. Eating breakfast	I will eat slowly and enjoy the food. I will not watch television or read the paper as I eat.
2. Driving to work	I will use traffic jams as an opportunity to practice breathing and driving mindfully.

Regular Activity	Mindful Activity
1._____	_____ _____
2._____	_____ _____
3._____	_____ _____
4._____	_____

LOOKING DEEPLY—GAINING INSIGHT

BY LIVING IN THE HERE AND now, we have an opportunity to stop, observe, and look deeply at our thinking, feeling, sensing, and experiencing. When we do so, every encounter has profound meaning. Each person we meet and every action we take offers an opportunity for personal growth and insight.

As your practice of daily mindfulness progresses, you will find you come to understand the *meaning* behind your thoughts, feelings, sensations, and experiences. There's an old legend about a man who made a periodic journey to purchase supplies in a city several hundred miles away. His only mode of transportation was walking. After making the round trip, he discovered a colony of ants on the cardamom seeds he had purchased. He carefully packed the seeds and made the trip back across the desert to the merchant from whom he had purchased them. His intent was not to exchange the seeds but to return the ants to their rightful home. It sounds a bit silly or farfetched, and yet, how refreshing it is to be reminded of the importance of looking at things so deeply that a person could demonstrate such compassion for the tiniest of creatures.

In the process of looking deeply, you begin to live your life in a more insightful, rather than robotic, way. Stopping to explore thoughts, feelings, sensations, and bodily experiences offers an individual a deep form of therapy. Whenever I have been able to stop, find a quiet environment, and retreat into myself, profound changes take place. Some of my best insights have come from quiet walks along the ocean, hiking in the mountains, and even in my own quiet space at home. Away from the everyday sounds of television, radio, stereos, traffic, and people, you can discover a new relationship with yourself. Most people are literally afraid of this kind of quiet, since they have not developed a way to be comfortable with themselves. Mindfulness is a process that, rather than creating fear, provides a technique for witnessing those aspects of life that create fear.

When appropriate, take some time to try the following exercises.

1. Look deeply at a thought you are experiencing. **Be** with the thought.

Why this thought? What does it mean? Why do I always seem to be focused on this thought?

2. Look deeply at a feeling you are experiencing. **Be** with the feeling.

If the feeling could talk, what would it say to you?

3. Look deeply at one sensation in your body. **Be** with the sensation.

If your body could talk, what would it say?

4. Look deeply at a person you care about. **Accept** this person completely in this moment.

What is it that you really value in this individual?

5. Overall, *stop* and *observe* and *look deeply* at your moment-by-moment behavior. Everyday activities, such as eating, speaking, and working, often take place without thought or consideration. In the process of looking deeply, you will begin to see the interconnectedness between every action and between all being.

THE ULTIMATE CHALLENGE of practicing mindfulness is to gain insight into yourself and your world moment by moment. Your individual practice of being mindful can have an effect on everyone. As you learn to look deeply, it becomes clear that no man is an island. Every action of yours has a profound impact on those around you, and literally on the whole universe.

Since I began embracing mindfulness, I have become more conscious of the impact that I have on the environment. I am more likely to recycle, and I avoid using products that may create a negative impact on the planet. I have made positive changes in my diet and eating habits and live a more simple life overall. All of these changes were the result of looking deeply at the potential consequence of each of my behaviors. When asked, "What is the greatest message we can leave for others?" Gandhi said simply, "My life is my message."

Reflections

The moment one gives close attention to anything, even a blade of grass, it becomes a mysterious, awesome, indescribably magnificent world in itself.
—HENRY MILLER

Understanding is the fruit of looking deeply.
—THICH NHAT HANH

- In what ways can I look more deeply today?

CREATING A MINDFUL WORKPLACE

THE POWER AND BEAUTY OF practicing mindfulness in our day-to-day lives is obvious to those dedicated to this practice. However, it can be a wonderful challenge to attempt to incorporate the mindfulness practice into the workplace environment where the concept may be unfamiliar and individuals find themselves caught up in the demands, changes, relationships, and the sometimes depersonalized nature of their workspace. As a college professor and consultant in a wide variety of professional environments, I have created an approach that can be useful to those working within any group or organization.

TEN PRINCIPLES FOR DEVELOPING A MINDFUL ORGANIZATION

Let Go.
Let go of any attachment to one system of working or managing in order to learn and rediscover what is best for everyone.

Open Your Heart.
Develop sensitivity to and compassion for the difficulties and pain of others. What affects one, affects all.

Simplify.
Eliminate the clutter besetting your body, mind, and spirit.

Forgive.
Do not hold on to anger, resentment, and negativity, as it leads to personal and professional disharmony and creates unfinished business.

Be Mindful.
The best gift you can give to others is your true presence.

Breathe!
Use mindful breathing to return to the present moment and regain composure, peace, and understanding.

Speak from Your Heart.
Use truth as the basis of your communication. Become aware of how your words affect the spirit and morale of your colleagues and your organization.

Think Health.
Develop and follow a plan to cultivate personal and organizational health.

Appreciate Others.
Recognize, respect, and support the good work and accomplishments of others.

Look Deeply.
Continuously examine your daily words and actions to be sure they are in harmony with your core values.

IF ONLY ONE PERSON in any working environment chooses to be more mindful, they can empower their colleagues and entire work group by their peaceful and healing presence. What better way to improve the bottom line?

Reflections

Mindfulness is how you love yourself. Loving your neighbor is done through mindful acts of compassion.
—CLAUDE WHITMYER

When we have inner peace, we can be at peace with those around us.
—THE DALAI LAMA

- Explore ways in which you will apply mindfulness to your daily work activities. How do you plan to be more mindful during your commute, with colleagues, during breaks, while using the computer, in working with others, during routine activities? How might you introduce this concept to your colleagues?

WHAT'S IT
ALL ABOUT?
MOMENT BY MOMENT

O N A RECENT TRIP TO Hawaii, I met a playwright who had written numerous Broadway and Hollywood productions. While having coffee together, I asked him if he had any secrets to share about writing. He replied, "People go to a play, or movie, or read books with the hope of getting at least one thought or inspiration. People typically will ask their friends, 'What was it all about?'" In his writing, he hopes to leave his readers with at least one message that will add to their lives.

So what is mindfulness really all about?

MINDFULNESS . . .

- is experiencing the body, mind, and spirit in the same place at the same time. It is an awareness of the present moment and of your activity in that moment.

- is being open to more than one perspective and living with an awareness that the ways of the past may not always be the best for the present.

- is learning to *experience* what is, instead of *resisting* what is.

- can help you reduce stress, increase productivity, enhance relationships, and be the basis of creating joy in life.

- incorporates an awareness of breathing as the vehicle used to call attention to the present moment, to renew the body, and to quiet the mind.

- is knowing your purpose.

- is learning to "witness" rather than react.

- is coming back to the present moment by moment.

Reflections

Shadows of the past are vague, and the future is too
distant to come into focus. Now is brightly illuminated
and richly colored. Today I will remember to
keep my mind in the present.
Now is all I have. Now is all anyone has.
—JUDITH GARRISON

Yesterday is but a dream, tomorrow is but a vision.
But today well lived makes every yesterday a dream of
happiness, and every tomorrow a vision of hope. Look
well, therefore, to this day.
—SANSKRIT PROVERB

The gift of life with all its joy and splendor is in the
moment at hand. Now it is ours to relish and enjoy;
now it is ours to cherish and to hold,
but only for the moment.
—ADOLFO QUEZADA

The past is past, and the future is yet to come. That
means the future is in your hands—the future entirely
depends on the present. That realization gives you a
great responsibility.
—THE DALAI LAMA

Bibliography

Andrews, Frank. *The Art and Practice of Loving.* Los Angeles: Jeremy P. Tarcher, Inc., 1991.

Beck, Charlotte Joko. *Everyday Zen: Love and Work.* New York: Harper Collins, 1989.

Borysenko, Joan. *Minding the Body, Mending the Mind.* Reading, Mass.: Addison Wesley, 1987.

Brandon, David. *Zen in the Art of Helping.* New York: Arakana, 1990.

Carlson, Richard, and Benjamin Shield. *Healers on Healing.* Los Angeles: Jeremy P. Tarcher, Inc., 1989.

Cooper, David A. *Silence, Simplicity, and Solitude.* New York: Bell Tower, 1992.

Csikszentmihalyi, Mihaly. *Flow: The Psychology of Optimal Experience.* New York: Harper & Row, 1990.

Cummings, Charles. *The Mystery of the Ordinary.* New York: Harper & Row, 1982.

Dass, Ram. *Be Here Now.* New York: Crown, 1971.

DeAngelis, Barbara. *Real Moments.* New York: Bantam Books, Inc., 1994.

Fields, Rick, *et al. Chop Wood, Carry Water.* Los Angeles: Jeremy P. Tarcher, Inc., 1984.

Goldberg, Natalie. *A Long Quiet Highway.* New York: Bantam Books, Inc., 1994.

Goldstein, Joseph. *Insight Meditation: The Practice of Freedom.* Boston: Shambhala Publications, 1993.

Goldstein, Joseph, and Jack Kornfield. *Seeking the Heart of Wisdom: The Path of Insight Meditation.* Boston: Shambhala Publications, 1987.

Goleman, Daniel, and Tara Bennett-Goleman. *The Meditative Mind: The Varieties of Meditative Experience.* Los Angeles: Jeremy P. Tarcher, Inc., 1988.

Gunaratana, Henepola. *Mindfulness in Plain English.* Boston: Wisdom Publications, 1993.

Halifax, Joan. *Fruitful Darkness: Reconnecting with the Body of the Earth.* San Francisco: Harper, 1993.

Hanh, Thich Nhat. *The Long Road Turns to Joy: A Guide to Walking Meditation.* Berkeley: Parallax Press, 1996.

———. *Living Buddha, Living Christ.* New York: Riverhead Books, 1995.

———. *Zen Keys.* New York: Doubleday, 1995.

———. *The Blooming of a Lotus: Guided Meditation Exercises for Healing and Transformation.* Boston: Beacon Press, 1993.

———. *Peace Is Every Step.* New York: Bantam Books, 1991.

———. *Present Moment, Wonderful Moment.* Berkeley: Parallax Press, 1990.

———. *Our Appointment with Life.* Berkeley: Parallax Press, 1990.

———. *The Sun, My Heart.* Berkeley: Parallax Press, 1988.

———. *Breathe! You Are Alive.* Berkeley: Parallax Press, 1988.

———. *Being Peace.* Berkeley: Parallax Press, 1987.

———. *The Miracle of Mindfulness.* Boston: Beacon Press, 1987.

Jackson, Phil. *Sacred Hoops: Spiritual Lessons of a Hardwood Warrior.* New York: Hyperion, 1995.

Johnson, Spencer. *Precious Present.* New York: Doubleday, 1984.

Kabat-Zinn, Jon. *Wherever You Go There You Are.* New York: Little, Brown & Co., 1995.

Kavanaugh, James. *Search.* San Francisco: Harper & Row, 1985.

Keating, Thomas. *Open Mind, Open Heart.* New York: Continuum Publishing Co., 1994.

Kornfield, Jack. *A Path with Heart.* New York: Bantam Books, 1993.

Kornfield, Jack, and Paul Breitzer. *A Still Forest Pool.* Wheaton, Ill.: Theosophical Publishing House, 1985.

Langer, Ellen. *Mindfulness.* Reading, Mass.: Addison Wesley, 1989.

Levine, Stephen. *A Gradual Awakening.* New York: Anchor-Doubleday, 1979.

Levine, Stephen. *Guided Meditations, Explorations, and Healing.* New York: Anchor, 1991.

Pennington, Basil. *Centered Living.* New York: Image, 1986.

Reid, Clyde. *Celebrate the Temporary.* New York: Harper & Row, 1972.

Salzberg, Sharon. *Loving Kindness: The Revolutionary Art of Happiness.* Boston: Shambhala Publications, 1995.

Sinetar, Marsha. *Do What You Love, the Money Will Follow.* New York: Paulist Press, 1987.

St. James, Elaine. *Inner Simplicity: 100 Ways to Regain Peace and Nourish Your Soul.* New York: Hyperion, 1995.

———. *Simplify Your Life: 100 Ways to Slow Down and Enjoy the Things That Really Matter.* New York: Hyperion, 1994.

Suzuki, Shunryu. *Zen Mind, Beginner's Mind.* New York: Weatherhill, 1986.

Tart, Charles T. *Living the Mindful Life: A Handbook for Living in the Present Moment.* Boston: Shambhala Publications, 1994.

Valles, Carlos G. *Courage to Be Myself.* New York: Doubleday, 1989.

Wellwood, John. *Ordinary Magic: Everyday Life as Spiritual Path.* Boston: Shambhala Publications, 1992.

Whitmyer, Claude. *Mindfulness and Meaningful Work: Explorations in Right Livelihood.* Berkeley: Parallax Press, 1994.

Wilber, Ken. *No Boundaries.* Boston: Shambhala Publications, 1985.

ABOUT
THE
AUTHOR

J ERRY BRAZA, PH.D., HAS spent over twenty years as a university professor with multi-disciplinary training in health and psychology. Presently he is teaching at Western Oregon State College and consults with a variety of organizations and companies nationwide. He is continually seeking creative ways to introduce the beauty of mindfulness into the personal and professional lives of others by not only teaching but modeling the practice itself. He is motivated and encouraged by the words of Gandhi, "My life is my message." In recent years he has worked with over ten thousand health professionals and employees in over two hundred companies and organizations. Personally he has been studying mindfulness with Thich Nhat Hanh and frequently visits his retreat center in Plum Village, France.

Jerry and his wife Kathleen recently moved to a beautiful and peaceful environment in Oregon where they find time to take mindful walks along the shore of the Willamette River. Living close to nature, they are exploring ways to live their life more simply and deliberately in the present moment. Kathleen is a counselor, writer, and professional clown. Jerry has two adult children, Mark and Andrea.

FOR ADDITIONAL INFORMATION on lectures, workshops, and seminars offered by Dr. Braza, contact

> HEALING RESOURCES
> P.O. Box 95
> Independence, OR 97351
> 1-800-473-HEAL (4325)
> e-mail: brazaj@fsa.wosc.osshe.edu

For information about books by Thich Nhat Hanh, contact

> PARALLAX PRESS
> P.O. Box 7355
> Berkeley, CA 94707

To subscribe to the *Mindfulness Bell,* a quarterly publication dedicated to mindful living, and to learn more about the teaching of Thich Nhat Hanh, contact

> COMMUNITY OF MINDFUL LIVING
> P.O. Box 7355
> Berkeley, CA 94707
>
> Phone (510) 527-3751
> Fax (51O) 525-7129
> e-mail: parapress@aol.com
> website: http://www.parallax.org